MW01629221

Small-Group Leader Training Program

Participant Workbook

Amy Jackson

ISBN-10: 1-61407-238-8
ISBN-13: 978-1-61407-238-6

Published by SmallGroups.com
Christianity Today
465 Gundersen Drive
Carol Stream, IL 60188
(630) 260-6200

Credits
Edited by: Amy Jackson
Design by: Jillian Hathaway

Are You Ready for an Adventure?

It was musty in the basement of our dorm, and the smell of burnt popcorn lingered in the air. We sat on old couches with rough wooden armrests, clutching our Bibles and nervously sizing up the other group members. The leader joyfully welcomed us and passed around a stack of paint swatches from the home improvement store, telling us to choose any swatch we liked. Once everyone held a small painted square, the leader asked, “How does the color you chose represent your personality?” We all let out a nervous chuckle, then stared blankly at our leader. She started by explaining how the color yellow was like her sunny personality. She was always looking for the bright side of things. Her warm smile definitely reminded me of the sun. One by one, we each shared, and I learned a lot that night about my fellow group members. At the end of the semester, I was having a hard time leaving this group of people who had once been strangers. I’d made a lifelong friend, and I’d studied the Book of James for the first time. I was hooked on this small group thing. Frankly, I couldn’t imagine not being in a small group after that. A few months later when I was asked to begin leading groups of my own, I jumped at the opportunity to create safe places for others to learn and grow.

Because you’re reading this, my guess is that you have a similar story of being changed by a small group. You learned something important or met true friends or found your way back to God. When we experience the loving, growing, healthy community that God designed us for, we can’t help but share it with others. As small-group leaders, we have the incredible opportunity to create meaningful group experiences for others to encounter God, build relationships, and grow in countless ways. This is the beautiful and fulfilling ministry of leading small groups.

My prayer is that as you go through the Small-Group Leader Training Program, you’ll be encouraged and equipped to lead your group with confidence. You’ll hear from small group experts who know what you’re going through and can share practical wisdom that you can apply right away. As you work through the questions and activities in this book with other leaders, you’ll learn from each other and form friendships with people who can continue to support you as a small-group leader. May you embark on this adventure of leading with confidence, humility, and a passion for working alongside the Holy Spirit. As you do, know that I’m cheering you on.

Amy

Amy Jackson
Managing Editor of SmallGroups.com

Table of Contents

Notes

1. Initial Session to Leaders
Hospital
①
②
③

2. Fitness Center 1 Thess. 5:11
① aerobic kneeling - pray together
② Pumping Scriptural Iron - read/study
③ Encouragement Drills - encourage each other

3. Family Gathering Phil 4:4-5
① Celebrate
- prayers answered
- Salvation
② A Family Gathering
- Bdays
- grads
- etc.

③ Launching Pad for Ministry
1 Peter 4:10

What are your spiritual gifts.

(4.) Laboratory for Leadership - developing leadership skills in your group members
1 Peter 5:2

Encourage group members to
lead prayer
lead questions
If that's their Gift.

www.nlbc.church
choose Wednesday night msgs.
Refuel Leaders

Session #1: Your Turn

Start It Out

What personal small-group experiences have encouraged you to become a small-group leader?

Talk It Out

Answer these questions in a group:

1. Think back to Stephanie. How would you respond to her in one or two sentences?

2. Why do you think it's so difficult to speak reality to each other?

3. What keeps people from fully engaging in small groups?

4. Small groups aren't just a place to be cared for; they're a place to minister to others and test our wings for leadership. What can you do to encourage this mutual service in your small group?

Live It Out

What are your top three takeaways from this video and discussion? What will you implement right away?

Further Resources

Training
Small-Group Leader Orientation Guide, SmallGroups.com

Books
The Irresistible Community, Dr. Bill Donahue

5 Images

1. Hospital that promotes healing – small Grp. supports
Gal 6:2 Bear one another's burdens

a. Rehab Care – who will walk with that family post hospital.

b. Confession Piece – Accountability, carry burden

2. Fitness center – Buddy system

2

Session #2

Healthy Leaders Lead Healthy Groups

Learn what Jesus teaches us about being good shepherds.

Jen Oyama Murphy is a former small-group director and support and recovery ministry director. She loves working as a lay counselor and bringing care into stories of trauma and harm. She is currently working on a master's in clinical psychology.

Notes

Session 2 Lead transformational Meetings.

IceBreaker Questions: what item in kitchen describes your personality.

Prayer

Session #2: **Your Turn**

Start It Out

We're giving you time for personal reflection. Find a comfortable spot where you won't be distracted. You may want to move away from the rest of the group a bit. Start the time by praying that God will speak to you and bring you clarity. Then read through the following questions, and honestly answer. Write your thoughts in the space provided. If it helps, take a look at Psalm 23 to get started.

1. How close do you feel to the Good Shepherd right now?

2. What helps you connect with God? Walks in the woods? Listening to music? Journaling? Reading your Bible?

3. How has God gifted you to be a small-group leader? What strengths do you bring to this role?

4. What's your motivation for leading a group? Is it healthy?

5. As you head into leading a small group, how are you feeling? Are you excited? Nervous? Are you dreading the first night? Why?

Talk It Out

Answer these questions in a group:

1. What's one takeaway from your time of personal reflection?

2. What do you think happens to the group when you lead like a good shepherd rather than a thief or a hired hand?

3. What are some warning signs to watch for that you're leading like a thief? A hired hand?

4. What are some signs that you're leading as a good shepherd?

5. What are some practical examples of how you could lead a small group as a good shepherd?

Live It Out

What are your top three takeaways from this video and discussion? What will you implement right away?

Further Resources

Training

Avoiding Burnout, SmallGroups.com
Healthy Leadership, SmallGroups.com
Shepherding Group Members, SmallGroups.com
Spiritual Disciplines for Leaders, SmallGroups.com

Books

Daring Greatly, Brené Brown
The Emotionally Healthy Leader, Peter Scazzero
Strengthening the Soul of Your Leadership, Ruth Haley Barton

3

Session #3

Lead a Transformational Meeting

Implement the four elements of great meetings.

Carter Moss is a campus pastor and life groups director for Newbreak Church, a large multi-site church in San Diego, California. He is passionate about building meaningful relationships and serving missionally in his community.

Notes

Session #3: Your Turn

Start It Out

Asking great questions is an important skill for small-group leaders. As a group, come up with a variety of questions you could use based on James 1:1–18. Read the passage aloud together. Then come up with at least three questions for each type below.

Open-Ended Questions

Think: Why? How? In what ways?
Steer clear of questions with yes/no answers or with only one answer.

Thought-Provoking Questions

Dig deeper than the safe, obvious answers.
Play devil's advocate to see issues from another perspective.

Practical Questions

Help group members apply what they're learning.
How are they changed, or how do they hope to change?

Talk It Out

Answer these questions in a group:

1. Make a list of at least three icebreakers you could use for just about any topic.

2. A group member has just shared a vulnerable story about feeling like he doesn't have enough faith. What follow-up questions might you ask to understand the issue?

3. Why do you think it's important for questions to "build" from more general to application?

4. All night your group is giving only "Sunday school answers." They're technically correct, but they're not adding to a lively discussion. What could you do to take the conversation deeper?

5. You've got 30 minutes left in your meeting and you realize you've only gotten through two questions in your guide. There are still eight to go. What do you do to keep great conversation going while moving ahead in the study?

6. What makes you nervous about leading a meeting? Is there a certain aspect that you're unsure of?

Live It Out

What are your top three takeaways from this video and discussion? What will you implement right away?

Further Resources

Training

Bible Study Methods for Groups, SmallGroups.com

Leading 101, SmallGroups.com

Theological Discussions for Everyone, SmallGroups.com

Books
Field Guide for Small Group Leaders, Sam O'Neal
Leading Life-Changing Small Groups, Dr. Bill Donahue
Leading Small Groups in the Way of Jesus, M. Scott Boren

4

Session #4

Build Authentic Relationships

Explore how to invest relationally in group members.

Carolyn Taketa is the executive director of small groups at Calvary Community Church in Westlake Village, California. She is a prominent voice in the small-group movement.

Notes

Session #4: Your Turn

Start It Out

When have you experienced a group that was authentic like the one described?

____

____

____

____

Talk It Out

Answer these questions in a group:

1. Why do you think we're tempted to keep the masks on in small groups?

____

____

____

____

2. The "one another" passages sound so nice, but they're really hard to live out. Why do you think it's so difficult?

____

____

____

3. One of your group members is having a serious surgery next week and will spend two nights in the hospital. What might your group do to care for her?

____

____

____

4. How can you keep in contact with your group members in between meetings? What things could you do weekly? Monthly? Quarterly? Annually?

____

____

5. What can you do to keep prayer a focus in your group—both praying for each other and praying together?

6. Are you comfortable sharing vulnerably with your group? Why or why not?

7. What are a few ground rules you might present to your group members to set the tone for an authentic group?

Live It Out

What are your top three takeaways from this video and discussion? What will you implement right away?

Further Resources

Training

Develop Real Relationships, SmallGroups.com
Making Small Groups Fun!, SmallGroups.com
Shepherding Group Members, SmallGroups.com

Books

Field Guide for Small Group Leaders, Sam O'Neal
Leading Small Groups in the Way of Jesus, M. Scott Boren
Life Together in Christ, Ruth Haley Barton

5

Session #5

When Groups Get Messy

Gain advice for the tricky parts of group life.

Bill Search is a leading voice in the small-group movement. His book, *Simple Small Groups,* has been used widely to help church leaders establish healthy patterns for small groups. Bill has vast experience, having served churches ranging from 2,000 to 20,000 in attendance.

Notes

Session #5: Your Turn

Start It Out

Read through the following group situation and apply what you've just learned. How would you handle this messy situation?

Your group has been meeting for three months, and you've started to build great friendships with each other. For the last three weeks, though, you've noticed a change in the energy of your group. Last month you started reading through the Book of Ephesians together, but you haven't gotten very far. And as each week goes by, you notice less enthusiasm for your study. The plan was to read one chapter a week and get through the entire book in six weeks. This is your fourth week reading Ephesians, though, and you're only on chapter two.

Your conversation about Jews and Gentiles has taken a lot longer than expected. Ava keeps asking questions about their differences and why they didn't get along. Every time Ava asks a question, Joe is quick to respond, but he talks for a long time without actually answering Ava's questions. Actually, now that you think of it, Joe talks a lot about all sorts of things. Last week he spent 30 minutes sharing about his fishing trip, and the week before that he kept showing pictures of his grandchildren throughout the meeting, which kept disrupting your discussion.

When you finally do end the discussion time and head into prayer time, though, you have another issue. Vanessa keeps bursting into tears as she shares her prayer requests—and then she talks about her issues way past the time group is supposed to end. You don't want to interrupt her while she's crying, though. It feels too awkward. What can you do to address these group issues?

Talk It Out

Answer these questions in a group:

1. Which of the messy scenarios in the video make you most nervous as a leader? Why?

2. When have you seen these messy situations handled poorly in groups? When have you seen them handled well?

3. What kind of group member are you? Do you tend to talk a lot or a little? Are you there early every meeting, or do you miss from time to time? Do you share too deeply, or do you stay on the surface?

4. How can you gain compassion for the people in your group who will be the opposite of you?

5. What are three things you can do to make your group a safe place for everyone to participate?

Live It Out

What are your top three takeaways from this video and discussion? What will you implement right away?

____

____

____

____

____

____

Further Resources

Training

Conquer Common Meeting Problems, SmallGroups.com
Handling Conflict in Small Groups, SmallGroups.com
Healthy Boundaries for Small Groups, SmallGroups.com
Ministering to Difficult Group Members, SmallGroups.com

Books

Field Guide for Small Group Leaders, Sam O'Neal
Leading Life-Changing Small Groups, Dr. Bill Donahue
Walking the Small Group Tightrope, Dr. Bill Donahue and Russ Robinson

Appendix

Why Small Groups?

The reason behind intentional Christian community

Carolyn Taketa

Churches use all sorts of names for small groups—life groups, growth groups, home groups, cell groups. They also use various models, numerous strategies for connection, various plans for assimilation, and church-specific vision and goals for their group ministries. Yet all would agree that small groups are a means to an end, not an end in and of themselves. Small groups exist as a way for people to engage in biblical community that helps them become more like Jesus in every area of their lives. The following are a few key biblical foundations, ministry purposes, and benefits of small groups.

Biblical Basis for Small Groups

God himself is in a community of three persons in one—the Father, Son, and Holy Spirit—who exist in perfect unity. So it is not surprising that from the beginning, God created us to be in community with one another. Genesis 2:18 states: “It is not good for man to be alone.” This passage is often used in the context of marriage, but it also speaks to our fundamental need to connect with others in the human community. What is striking about this statement is that God makes it before the Fall. There’s no sin yet and no disobedience; man is in perfect intimacy with God. And yet, God declares that man is alone and that it is not good. Dr. Gilbert Bilezikian points out in *Community 101:*

> Community is deeply grounded in the nature of God. It flows from who God is. Because he is community, he creates community. It is his gift of himself to humans. Therefore, the making of community may not be regarded as an optional decision for Christians. It is a compelling and irrevocable necessity, a binding divine mandate for all believers at all times.

When Jesus’ ministry began, he called 12 disciples to be his primary relational and ministry community. Did Jesus need this motley crew to help him? Not really. But Jesus chose to love them, teach them, and pour himself into relationships with them, thereby creating the first “small group.”

The apostles continued Jesus’ model and formed a community of believers who loved God and loved one another. Despite incredible persecution and against all odds, this ragtag group of Jesus-followers launched small communities (i.e. church) that proclaimed the gospel and changed the world forever.

Purpose of Small Groups

When we look at the early church we get a picture of small communities of people who followed Jesus together. The Book of Acts, especially Acts 2:42–47, gives us a great picture of the early church and the components of biblical community, which encompassed both the "temple courts" and "house to house."

These believers engaged in life together through teaching, fellowship, communion, prayer, miracles, radical generosity, and corporate worship. They spent time together eating, learning, celebrating, proclaiming the Good News, and supporting each other. In addition, the 50-plus "one another" verses in the New Testament flesh out other aspects of this community. For example, it was a place where people loved, forgave, served, bore burdens, encouraged, exhorted, prayed, equipped, spoke truth in love, confessed sins, and treated each other as precious members of one body.

God never intended for us to live the Christian life alone. How can we apply these "one another" references unless we are in intentional, close relationships with each other? God calls us to love, not in an abstract or superficial way, but in a deep, face to face, life-on-life, transformative way—which is difficult and inevitably messy.

In our modern culture, small groups are often viewed merely as a program or a fellowship ministry within the church. But for the New Testament church, it was a way of life, encompassing every area of their lives. Their relationships with one another were critical to their pursuit of Jesus, their growth in Christ, and their witness to the Good News. It would be impossible to experience biblical community apart from spiritually significant, intentional relationships with other believers. Relational structures like small groups, therefore, are an integral part of "being" the church and not just "doing" church.

Character Change Happens Best in the Context of Community

The consumer mentality rampant in our culture has permeated our understanding of community. We focus on what we are going to get out of church or small group rather than what God is going to do in us and through us because of our relationships within community. We need each other to help us know the truth about who we are, who God is, and how we can live in light of those truths. Like iron sharpening iron, the relationships we form within our small communities can become a tool for God to use in our character transformation. Dr. Bilezikian writes:

> It is in small groups that people can get close enough to know each other, to care and share, to challenge and support, to confide and confess, to forgive and be forgiven, to laugh and weep together, to be accountable to each other, to watch over each other and to grow together. Personal growth does not happen in isolation. It is the result of interactive relationships. Small groups are God's gift to foster changes in character and spiritual growth.

We live in an increasingly fragmented and disconnected world. Though social media and other technology have made our world seemingly more connected, people have fewer genuine friends than ever before. It feels scary and threatening to allow ourselves to be known or to invest in knowing someone else at a deep level. It is much easier and more convenient to stay on the surface. Yet when we take the risk of being authentic with a small group of people, we can experience God's grace and love coming through others, which leads to freedom and transformation.

John Ortberg writes in *The Me I Want to Be*: "God uses people to form people. That is why what happens between you and another person is never merely human-to-human interaction—the Spirit longs to be powerfully at work in every encounter." So the goal of small groups is to create environments where Spirit-driven, life-giving experiences can flourish. While the type of group or study can help promote a positive environment, the real things that promote a healthy environment for flourishing are prayer, support, service, confession, worship, accountability, conflict resolution, social gatherings, and simply doing life together. Regardless of the specific guidelines a church may have in its small-group ministry, its objective ultimately is to help people engage in relationships that help them become more like Christ. Spend time building an environment that allows true relationships to flourish.

Small Groups Are on a Mission Beyond Themselves

The Great Commission in Matthew 28:19–20 mandates that every follower of Christ is on mission to "go and make disciples of all nations." Jesus gave this instruction to all his followers, both as individuals and as the body of Christ. We, as a small group and as a church, bear collective witness to the good news of Jesus Christ.

One of Jesus' final instructions to his disciples is found in John 13:34–35: "A new command I give you: Love one another. As I have loved you, so you must love one another. By this everyone will know that you are my disciples, if you love one another." Note that Jesus did not say people will know we are Christians by how many churches we build, how many Bible studies we complete, how many prayers we say, or how many people come to our church. The litmus test is clear: people will know we are Christ-followers when we love each other the way Jesus does.

Theologian Francis Schaeffer asserted, "Our relationship with each other is the criterion the world uses to judge whether our message is truthful—Christian community is the final apologetic." Our non-believing friends, family, co-workers, and neighbors are watching and deciding on the validity of the gospel message. We need others to help us live lives worthy of God's calling so that people will see the power of God's love in and through us.

Ultimately, small groups are a way of living out our purpose, both as individuals and as a collective group of believers—to be the church. We share a common foundation of faith and God has called us to live out the implications of that faith in a relational community, in the context that we call a small group.

CAROLYN TAKETA is Executive Small Groups Director at Calvary Community Church in Westlake Village, California.

Three Keys for New Leaders

What I learned by falling down the stairs

Peri Gilbert

It was my first day of high school when I spotted him: Prince Charming. He totally distracted me as I was going up the steps. Like the classic scene in every romantic comedy and sitcom, I fell, papers flying everywhere. As I gathered my books and my pride, I learned several lessons that have served me well over the years. And I hope that you'll benefit from them, too.

1. Watch Where You're Going

Don't lose focus as you lead your group. Small groups are for personal and spiritual growth. They are designed to help people not only build relationships with each other, but also build or enhance their relationship with Christ. Your focus, then, is to spur that growth.

Matthew 28:19 tells us that we are to "go and make disciples." God gives us the most amazing opportunity as small-group leaders to do this through our groups. It's a natural environment in which we can love and encourage people.

As a team, you work toward the common goals of personal and spiritual growth. Teams do not survive without a goal or working together. If one person decides to act on his or her own, he or she takes the chance of tripping up the stairs. Therefore, working together as the body of Christ, encourage and support one another so that the whole group is healthy and growing and full of love (Ephesians 4:16). As long as you remain focused and encourage your small group to stay focused, you will win the prize: amazing relationships and growth in Christ.

2. Get Rid of the Stairs

What unnecessary obstacles are in your way? As a new small-group leader, I clamped onto every "what if" available. What if my house is messy? What if I say the wrong thing? What if the members don't like me? What if I don't have an answer? I nearly "what iffed" myself and my group to death. Don't fall into that temptation.

One of the Enemy's most subtle tools is keeping you from moving forward by paralyzing you with fear and self-doubt. He has no desire for you to influence others for Christ. As you take the step to lead, doubts and fears very well may enter your mind and distract you from your purpose. However, there are ways to deflect these doubts and fears.

One way to rid yourself of negative thoughts is to fill yourself with God's Word. As Christians, we are in for a lifelong fight against the Devil's tricks. In order to fight, we have to be ready for the attacks (Ephesians 6:10–17).

So prepare yourself with God's Word. One thing I've done is placed Scripture on my bathroom mirror. I chose this location because it's one place I stand every day. While I'm doing my hair and makeup, I'm reading these truths: "Perfect love drives out fear" (1 John 4:18); "Therefore, there is now no condemnation for those who are in Christ Jesus" (Romans 8:1); "You were bought at a price" (1 Corinthians 6:20); "You are a chosen people, a royal priesthood, a holy nation, God's special possession." (1 Peter 2:9); "Now you are the body of Christ, and each one of you is a part of it" (1 Corinthians 12:27). You could also put Scripture on your dashboard or on your fridge. Put them where you will see them every day. God's Word is full of affirmations to dispute the fear and doubt we experience. The more you take in God's truths, the more these truths transform your mind (Romans 12:1–2), making you the leader God has called you to be.

Another way to get rid of unnecessary obstacles is to surround yourself with safe people with whom you can share your doubts and questions. My small-group coordinator was one of my greatest encouragements during my "what if" stage. He did not mind me asking all the stupid questions or expressing my fears. He gave me practical solutions for my worries and encouraged me to be a team leader. He invested in me.

If you do not have people around you encouraging you and building you up, you may need to evaluate who you're surrounding yourself with. Don't forget that we have been called to live abundantly and to help others do the same.

3. Help and Be Helped

It was great to have someone help me pick up my books that day I stumbled on those steps, but too often we're scared to ask for help. Even if you've been through a plethora of training and part of many small groups, you still may not have a clue how to handle situations that arise in your new group. Don't be embarrassed that you don't know. Now is the time to step up as a leader and ask for help.

A great leader is not the one who knows all the answers—those leaders feel they have nothing to learn. Instead, a great leader realizes he or she doesn't know it all and, for the sake of the team, asks for help. See what your coach or pastor has to say. When you're vulnerable with the group and let them know you don't have all the answers, you show them that it's okay not to know everything.

At the same time, don't forget to serve and help others (Romans 12:3–12). It's easy for a new leader's mind to translate leading into duty. You never want your small group to be a duty. The members in your group are children of God, and he has called you to serve them. Being a leader is a sacrificial position that changes lives. As you serve the members of your small group, you show them Christ. Remember his example: "The Son of Man did not come to be served, but to serve" (Matthew 20:28).

Not only do you have the opportunity to serve, but your small group does as well. Binding together as the body of Christ, you have the chance to serve, encourage, and love others together. As you change the 8 to 10 lives in your small group, those 8 to 10 lives, in turn, impact another 8 to 10 lives. What an amazing privilege!

As a new small-group leader, you will change lives. And as you apply this advice, as well as the advice from your small-group coach and pastor, you'll minimize the distractions and avoid future falls. Be confident in your call as a small-group leader and lead your heart out.

Peri Gilbert is the Small-Group Coordinator at The Simple Church in Bossier City, Louisiana.

Emphasize Relationships in Your Group

How to set the stage for real friendships

Mark Ingmire

When we talk about the key parts of a small group, we usually talk about the Bible study, sharing, prayer, group mission, or outreach. Because we see these as the most important elements, our leader training focuses on doing those things well. However, there's one part of group life that we don't pay as much attention to, yet has huge importance: relationships. Though we may spend little time training how to build, deepen, and maintain friendships within the group, we can't ignore them if we want groups to be healthy. And we can't assume they'll naturally develop.

Consider for a moment a small group without deep relationships. This group will be made up of simple acquaintances who don't do much to support one another. They'll hold in hurt and disagreements rather than seek to forgive wrongs committed against each other because they're not invested in the relationships. They won't respond to needs that are expressed, assuming someone else will take care of them. And they won't experience much life change together because depth and accountability simply aren't present.

Without a strong emphasis on relationships, the best thing a small group can do is impart head knowledge. That same knowledge, when discussed in an environment that promotes relationships, has the power to move from the head to the heart. Group members allow that knowledge to impact them, and they seek to apply it. That's when life change happens. So let's look at how we can model and emphasize healthy and life-changing relationships within small groups.

Make the Group Safe

You can establish a few guidelines during the group's discussion that will help foster relationships. Introduce these guidelines before you jump into your study time to help you model how a healthy, life-changing group functions.

Be Transparent

One of my greatest frustrations is group members who respond to questions with superficial answers. To help with this, you'll need to model transparent sharing, talking about your real needs, struggles, and frustrations. Your group can tell if you're being transparent or superficial, and they'll follow your lead. You may find that it isn't easy being transparent, but it's important to try. The more you practice, the easier it will be. Your transparency will give your group members permission to be transparent, sharing their true selves with the group. This is part of tilling the soil of relationships.

Don't Rescue

When people share an experience that has deeply impacted them, it's our tendency to try to make them feel better about the situation or about themselves. This is especially true if a group member gets emotional. I have heard people say, "God will use that situation," or, "It will be okay." Although both of these sentiments may be true, they quickly shut down further sharing. Rather than responding with these sentiments, allow time to pause and reflect, thank them for sharing, and perhaps respond by saying "I'm so sorry," or, "That sounds like a really tough situation."

This is especially important when group members have difficulty expressing themselves. Perhaps they're stuttering or searching for the words to express what they're thinking. Rather than allow them the space to sort it out and say what they're thinking and feeling, we try to rush in and rescue them by putting words into their mouths. We must recognize that this is because we feel uncomfortable, not because it's helpful to the people sharing. Rather than rush in to try to finish their thoughts for them, be patient and allow them to express themselves. After they've shared, you can always ask questions to clarify what they meant.

No Side Conversations

If you begin a side conversation while another person is sharing, it communicates that you're not listening and, worse, that you don't care about what's being said. When someone is sharing in the group, give your full attention to him or her. If group members try to start a side conversation with you, steer their attention to the person sharing with the group.

Don't Fix

Here are actual pieces of advice I've heard in small-group discussions:

- I think you should sue their pants off.
- You need to pray harder and read your Bible more.
- You need to just get over it.

Giving advice is extremely dangerous. First, the advice given is often bad advice. Second, the person sharing usually isn't asking for advice. Instead of giving advice, listen and ask follow-up questions to help the person unpack the situation. The best way to advance the conversation without giving advice is simply to recognize the situation's importance. Saying something like, "Wow, I'm so sorry you're in this situation," expresses your empathy and concern for the situation, yet doesn't give any advice.

A mistake group leaders often make is jumping in too early to say, "Let's pray about this." Realistically, not everyone is ready to pray about an issue they bring up. Rather than jump to conclusions about the best way to pray for the situation, ask follow-up questions that help the group member clarify the issue and better understand his or her thoughts and feelings. You might ask, "So how did that make you feel?" or, "What are your concerns with this situation?" Before heading to prayer, consider asking what the person would like prayer for. Too often the way we pray for others consists of giving advice. For instance, someone might pray, "Give Lauren the courage to speak up to Tony," when Lauren hasn't said anything about desiring to speak up to him. This kind of advice-giving will shut down the group member from sharing in the future.

Use "I" Statements

When group members use "we" in regards to how they feel or think, they remove themselves from the ownership of their statement. For instance, a group member might say, "We all struggle with forgiving others," in an effort to keep the conversation more surface-level. When we use the word "I," we take ownership. So, using our example, a group member should instead say, "I struggle to forgive my mom for what she's done." Using "I" statements communicates that you trust your fellow group members enough to be honest with them about your thoughts and feelings. If you model using "I" statements, your group members will follow suit.

We Don't All Have to Agree

Whenever people gather, there are bound to be disagreements—even if they're over silly things like the type of snacks to bring. For some reason, though, in small groups we often feel that we should all agree on everything. But that's simply not true. There's a big difference between sharing an opinion and trying to convince everyone else in the group that they should share your opinion. If group members feel others will just try to convince them of the "right" way to think, they won't share their own opinions. Remember that freedom to share is an indispensable part of being a small group. Without this safety, group members won't share, and you likely won't experience much life change together.

Learn to Really Listen

Pay attention to the group member who is sharing. Practice being an active listener. Show interest by keeping good eye contact, nodding your head, leaning slightly toward the speaker, and reflecting back to the group member what has been shared. Don't be distracted by texting, thinking up your next response, or watching the clock. Group members feel valued when they know that you're listening.

Stay In Touch Between Meetings

There are 168 hours in one week. If your group meets for 2 hours every week, there are 166 hours where life is happening for your group members. Every hour that passes separates group members a little more, which means you'll have to spend quite a bit of time reconnecting at each meeting.

While there's nothing wrong with taking time to reconnect at meetings, you can help minimize this dynamic by modeling how to keep in touch with group members between meetings and encouraging others to do the same. In order to do this, make sure group members have each other's contact information. That keeps you from being the bottleneck for developing relationships. If someone is absent from one of your group meetings, for instance, anyone in the group is able to contact him or her without having to get the information from you first.

Staying in touch between meetings also helps you prepare for future meetings. The conversations you have during the week will help you get to know your group members better which helps you know how best to lead. Your group members may feel more comfortable sharing with you or others individually rather than with the entire small group.

Care for Group Members

Talk is cheap. You can say that you care about your group members as much as you want, but if you never actually do anything to take care of them, your words won't mean anything. The axiom proves true: Actions speak louder than words.

In order for relationships to grow, you'll have to engage in meaningful acts of service. There are several simple things you can do as a leader to model and emphasize serving one another. It doesn't necessarily mean mowing their lawn or doing their laundry—unless that's what they really need. Rather, there are lots of simple things you can do to let people know you care.

Celebrate Birthdays

It may seem overly simple, but recognizing and celebrating group members' birthdays is a great way to care for them. Plus, it gives your group a reason to party, which is always fun. Don't pass up this easy way to serve your members.

Celebrate Special Occasions
Be attentive to what your small-group members are involved in outside of group life. When a group member graduates from school, gets a promotion, or earns recognition in your community, celebrate! Likewise, if group members are participating in a local play, coordinating a community event, or excelling on a sports league, attend their events and cheer them on. Being there for your group members' interests and achievements will go a long way in communicating that you care.

Have Dinner Together
Over the course of a few months, have each group member over to your home for a home cooked meal. Sharing a meal is a very personal way to build relationships with people in your group, and it helps them feel valued. Alternatively, invite pairs of group members over for dinner not only to develop your relationship with each of them but also to foster a relationship between the two group members.

Quickly Address Needs
When a group member expresses a need for help, don't let your only response be, "Let's pray about that." It's great to pray, but you'll also want to see if there's anything you or the group can do to help. If you're not sure what might help, ask.

As you begin to invest in relationships within your group, you'll see deeper sharing and more life change happening. Never underestimate the importance of healthy relationships in a group. If you want to see growth, you'll need to invest in relationships.

Mark Ingmire is the Adult Discipleship Director at Forest Hill Church's South Park Campus in Charlotte, North Carolina.

First Night Survival Guide

Preparing for and leading your first meeting

Will Johnston

Someone asked you to lead a small group. And right now, you're really questioning why you said yes. You've had some training, found a study, talked with your pastor or director, and even had a few people say they're coming. But now it's just two days before your first meeting, and you're not feeling very prepared. You find yourself panicking, wondering what you'll do if no one talks, or if your entire group is made up of weird people.

Leading a small group isn't rocket science, but it can be a bit intimidating, especially the first time around. Here are a few tips to make your first group meeting go smoothly—a survival guide, if you will.

Preparation

It's true: Failing to plan is planning to fail. So consider these four things while preparing for your first meeting.

Communication

A day or two before the group meeting, get in touch with the folks who have expressed interest in your group. You can use the phone, a text, social media, e-mail, or whatever works best for your context and demographic.

Be sure to remind everyone when and where the group is meeting and give them your phone number in case someone gets lost. On that note, be sure your phone is turned on and the ringer is turned up before the group starts. You don't want anyone to miss the meeting because they couldn't get in touch with you at the last minute.

You may also want to ask people to confirm whether or not they're coming so that you can be prepared. It can be tough both mentally and logistically if you expect 15 and get 5 (or vice versa).

Food

Nothing creates conversation like cuisine. I don't know if you've ever noticed, but strangers sitting around a table full of food are much more relaxed and talkative. Food breaks the ice and opens people up. My agenda for the first group meeting is often just dinner and conversation. I want people to start getting to know one another before we dive into a study.

If you don't think you're up for tackling dinner (and I'll be honest, cooking a whole meal for a group of people can add stress to the evening) be sure to have snacks. I recommend the three Cs: chips, cookies, and caffeine. In other words: something salty, something sweet, and something good to drink.

Environment

Create a welcoming environment. People are less likely to stick around if they're uncomfortable. Make sure you have enough chairs. Turn on the lights. Burn a candle to get rid of that funky odor. Put a fresh hand towel in the bathroom.

As a side note: There are some folks with the gift of hospitality reading this who have no idea why this section's here. For those of us without the gift of hospitality, or for those who are perhaps new to having a place to host (ahem, 23-year-old guys just out of college), these tips aren't always second-nature.

Prayer

Prayer is the easiest thing to overlook during the frantic preparation process, but it's also one of the most vital. This isn't just a social gathering or a team meeting. Your goal as a small-group leader is not only to create community but also to make disciples, to help people become more like Jesus. And if you're going to do that well, you'll need his help to do it.

In the days leading up to the first meeting, pray for your group. Pray that God would send the right people and that those who come would connect well and find community. Pray for wisdom and discernment for yourself as the group leader. Above all, pray that God would be glorified through your group.

Go Time

Once you've prepped as much as possible, you'll actually need to lead the meeting. Whatever you do, be sure to focus on community and vision.

Community

I'd argue that discipleship should be the top priority for your small group. However, it's not your top priority for the first meeting. Instead, your main goal is for people to get to know each other. You don't need to cover material or help people grow spiritually or any of that. Just make sure people actually connect with one another. That's what will bring them back and open the door for discipleship. Here are a few tips to help make that happen:

- Set aside time for conversation. Consider not having any other agenda for

the first meeting. Again, having conversation over dinner is a great option.
- Greet everyone personally. As the small-group leader, do your best to meet everyone at the door when they first come in, especially if they don't know others in the group.
- If you notice people standing alone, talk with them and introduce them to other folks. Help group members connect with each other.
- Use an icebreaker question like, "Tell us a story about your best friend from childhood." It may seem silly, but it helps spark conversation, and the right questions can really help a group get to know one another. (Check out other icebreakers on SmallGroups.com.)
- Help people learn each other's names. If it's a big group you may want to bring name tags. You could also play a game to help remember names. For instance, ask people to say their name and an adjective that describes them and begins with the same first letter (e.g., Serene Sarah, Theology Tony, Caring Cathy). Six years later, I still remember my friend Adam as "Average Adam" because he introduced himself that way.

Vision

While your first priority is building community, you have a very important second priority for the night: casting vision for the group. The people who are part of your group want to know what you'll be doing together.

Answer their questions by considering:
- Why are we meeting?
- What do we hope to accomplish?
- Are we a group that requires consistent attendance, or is it okay if people pop in and out?
- Do we have a group covenant?
- Will we have weekly homework?
- Are members expected to attend service projects?
- How long will the group last?

If your church has a set idea of what your group will be about, you'll simply communicate these expectations. If you have flexibility over what you'll be doing, studying, and accomplishing, you may want to involve everyone in answering these questions.

Remember that it's much easier to set these expectations at the beginning than it is to change the culture of the group later on. And if a problem does need to be addressed in the future, it's helpful if the expectations were communicated up front.

Next Steps

Whew! You made it through your first meeting. Even if you're exhausted and just want to watch some TV or go to bed, there are a couple of things you need to do that will help you a lot in the future. Then there are a few things you can do later to follow up.

Right Away

First of all, it's a good idea to do something to help you remember people's names. It's easy to forget them by week two. One helpful idea is to picture each person in your head and repeat his or her name (and adjective) a few times. Another idea that has helped me is to sit where you sat during the meeting and write down each person in the group by where they sat. Start with the person to your right and continue until you've made it all the way around the circle. Lastly, you may want to find your new group members on Facebook and send friend requests. All of these tips will help you remember your new group members' names.

Secondly, make a note to follow through on any requests. I've found that during the meeting I might tell one person I'd e-mail him and another person that I'd look up more information on the passage. Don't forget about these requests. Try to do them right away. If that's not possible, write yourself a reminder.

Later On

At some point in the next day or so, you should follow up with your new group members. You can use whatever communication medium is appropriate for your context. I personally find e-mail to be a great tool for the post-meeting follow up. Remind group members of any relevant details, especially the time of the next group meeting and any homework that needs to be done before then. You can also include a link to resources (books, studies, curriculum, etc.) that they need to order for the next meeting.

Lastly, continue to pray for your group. As you get to know them better and better, you'll know how to pray specifically for each member. Most important, ask Jesus to help you all follow him more closely.

Don't Stress Out

I would guess that you've been overwhelmed with information about leading a group, and you probably have no idea how to keep it all straight. Even this "survival guide" may seem overwhelming. You may be going overboard trying to get everything perfect before your first night. If that's you, I have some words of wisdom.

The first night of my small group was just last week. We aren't a new group, but it was our first meeting in a long time and we intentionally welcomed new people to our meeting. Unfortunately, the day of the meeting I didn't have time to prepare. Instead, I ended up dealing with a broken down car, figuring out how to carry a carful of stuff home on the subway. Once home I had to try to fix my cell phone charger, so that my phone would be charged before group. Plus, my wife and I had a fight—just to top off a great day.

Needless to say, very few of the things I normally do to prepare didn't happen. I even missed an e-mail from a prospective group member who wanted to come to my group. According to my suggestions for a successful first meeting, I failed.

But everything turned out fine. The group still met, and we still had a good time getting to know one another. And I don't think anyone hates me. Ultimately, we need to remember that God is responsible for his church, and that includes each of our small groups. God uses our preparations, but God will work it all out, even if you forget the cookies.

Will Johnston is the Director of Build Community at Eastside Christian Church in Anaheim, California.

5 Reasons to Quit Your Small Group

And why you might want to stick around.

Amy Jackson

Leading a small group is tiring. It's frustrating. And it's time-consuming. I'll even admit there are days I want to quit—nights that I get done with my small group and want to scream at how unproductive we were, or how much ground we lost, or how disruptive a particular group member was.

But there are also days when I can't sleep after small group because I'm so excited about what God's doing in our group. There are days when I feel more alive than I've ever felt because I see the body of Christ working together in our small group—through an impassioned intercessory prayer, a plan to scrape together resources to meet a need, or a breakthrough moment that overcomes sin's power in a group member's life.

The truth is, if God didn't call us to gather in community, life would be a lot easier without groups. It's a lot easier to go to work, drive home, and stay home. It's a lot easier to choose the people you hang out with—and stop hanging out with the people who make you uncomfortable. It's a lot easier to live out the "one another" commands when it's just you and your dog at home.

Community is hard work. And if it weren't for God calling us to gather, I'd say let's all quit. Right now.

But it's clear that we're supposed to gather. Even Jesus spent time gathering with others. Carolyn Taketa writes,

> When Jesus' ministry began, he called 12 disciples to be his primary relational and ministry community. Did Jesus need this motley crew to help him? Not really. But Jesus chose to love them, teach them, and pour himself into relationships with them, thereby creating the first "small group."
>
> The apostles continued Jesus' model and formed a community of believers who loved God and loved one another. Despite incredible persecution and against all odds, this rag tag group of Jesus-followers launched small communities (i.e. church) that proclaimed the gospel and changed the world forever.

Small groups carry out the mission of the church, and you—you!—get to be part of it. While it's an incredible honor to work alongside God as we lead our groups, it doesn't always feel like that. So here are a few reminders for when things get tough in your small group:

1. Community is hard.

Gather a group of sinful people in a sinful world, and it's no wonder that our small groups are a mess. But God works through the mess to change our hearts and lives. Through community, we become more Christlike. We are supported in this difficult life, and we have someone to celebrate with when God shows up in amazing ways. Without small groups, I doubt I would have found my way back to God, and I can guarantee that I wouldn't be the person I am today. Through small groups I have overcome sin, worked on unhealthy patterns of relating, and had people call me out on bad decisions. I've also developed life-long friends, grown closer to my husband, and learned helpful parenting skills. Community is hard, but boy is it worth it.

2. For every step forward, you take (at least) one back.

I love to see progress—whether it's the progress bar on a survey, the percentage read on my Kindle books, or checking items off my grocery list. I don't think I'm alone. So when we see that for every step our group takes forward, we take two steps back, it's no wonder we get frustrated. How will we ever reach the goal?

But in life transformation, change isn't linear. We step forward, circle back, head out on a side trail, and then find ourselves at a dead end. Rather than get down on ourselves for this sporadic and hard-to-measure change, let's learn to embrace the journey. After all, we know we'll never reach perfection this side of heaven. So let's celebrate little milestones, and let's learn from each step (and misstep) along the way.

3. Not every meeting leaves you energized and hopeful.

Sometimes we leave group feeling fully alive, excited about what God is doing in and through our group. That kind of excitement can inspire us to keep going. It can make us feel proud of our group, confident in our leadership, and excited about what God has next. But there are plenty of meetings that won't make us feel that way.

It's not healthy to base our joy on what's happening in our small group. We must find our joy in God alone. When I find myself fluctuating emotionally from meeting to meeting, I know it's time to focus on my personal health as a leader. I need to take care of myself and invest deeply in my relationship with Christ so that I'm not depending on the group for my joy. When my joy is grounded in Christ alone, I can roll with the highs and lows of group life, celebrating the successes and working to overcome the struggles.

4. You mess up.

I'm incredibly grateful to a campus minister who told me one of the best things I could do for my group members was tell them, "I don't know." Whether we feel the pressure from our coaches and pastors, or we place the pressure on ourselves, we too often believe that we must be perfect leaders who know everything and can handle every situation with ease. If you're a new leader, I need to tell you something: You are going to mess up. More than once. Maybe even in a big way. I'm sorry, but it's true. (Thanks for nodding along, veteran leaders.)

But I want you to know that it's okay to mess up. Really! It's a good idea to do things to the best of our ability as leaders, learning as we go, and asking our coaches for help when we need it. But we must also remember that God is bigger than any mistake we could make as we lead our groups.

And God may just be trying to teach us something. Leading a group is a great way to focus on your own spiritual development. I have grown more as a leader than I've ever grown as a participant. When you lead, you have to figure it out. You have to go through the issues rather than simply ignore them. And all that learning to handle hard stuff changes you for the better. I've never depended on God more than when I'm responsible for a small group of people.

5. You feel overwhelmed.

It doesn't take long for new leader excitement to turn to new leader regret: *There's no way I can handle this!* We suddenly realize how hard leading a group can be, the spiritual struggles of our group members, and how little we know, and we feel overwhelmed.

The good news is that feeling overwhelmed can be a catalyst to do two really healthy things: lean on God and empower others. During a particularly hard time in my life, I took up running. Every day when I ran, I reached the end of my strength, and it taught me to lean on God instead of my own strength. This daily reminder was what I needed to recognize my limited abilities and remind myself to depend on God. When we feel in over our heads, we are forced to learn the life-changing lesson of leaning on God.

On a practical level, we can also learn to empower others to lead so we're not doing it all ourselves. Too many leaders are happy to do it all—organize meetings, pick the study, ask the questions, and lead the prayer time. Pretty soon, the group members form an unhealthy dependence on us for their growth. They know we'll do it all, so they never exercise their spiritual gifts or strengths. Don't let your group members depend on you like this. Instead, empower them to lead in ways that match their gifts and strengths. Your group members will feel ownership for the group, and they'll help you lead in important ways. Plus, you won't feel so overwhelmed with all the tasks of leading. Together, you can lead a thriving small group.

If you're leading a small group, my guess is that you've experienced God's power through groups before. More than likely, you've personally been changed by a small group: you've been held accountable, learned something new from God's Word, or connected with others in a deep, life-changing way. Now you have the incredible honor of facilitating a group where others can experience those same things. It's not easy, but it's worth it. It's not simple, but it's incredibly good. Learn to lean on God, and he will guide you every step of the way.

Amy Jackson is managing editor of SmallGroups.com.

Made in the USA
Lexington, KY
23 June 2019